KIDS ON EARTH

Wildlife Adventures – Explore The World
The Atlantic Spotted- Dolphin

Sensei Paul David

COPYRIGHT PAGE

Kids On Earth: Wildlife Adventures - Explore The World

The Atlantic Spotted- Dolphin

by Sensei Paul David,

Copyright © 2023.

All rights reserved.

978-1-77848-217-5

KoE_WildLife_Amazon_PaperbackBook_Portugal_spotted dolphin

978-1-77848-216-8

KoE-Wild-Life-Amazon-eBook Portugal_spotted dolphin

978-1-77848-566-4

KoE_WildLife_Ingram_PaperbackBook_portugal_spotted dolphin

This book is not authorized for free distribution copying.

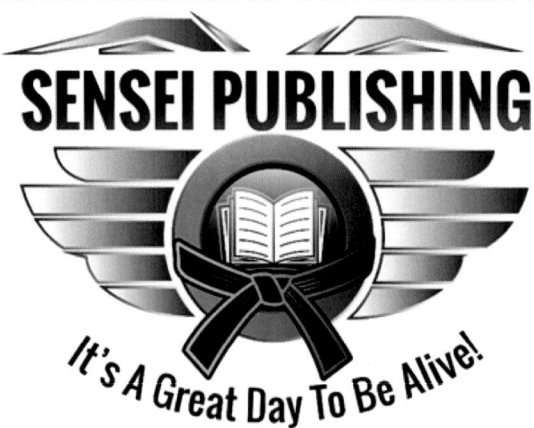

www.senseipublishing.com

@senseipublishing

#senseipublishing

Synopsis

The Atlantic spotted dolphin is an oceanic species that primarily inhabits the waters of Portugal and the Azores. This species is one of the most common dolphins seen in the area and has a unique spotted pattern on their bodies. Atlantic spotted dolphins travel in small pods of up to 20 individuals and are carnivorous, feeding on a variety of fish and squid. They are highly intelligent and capable of using echolocation and tools to help them hunt. This book provides 30 fun facts about the Atlantic spotted dolphin of Portugal, including their behavior, diet, and life cycle. It also provides an overview of their habitat, intelligence, and social structure.

Get Our FREE eBooks Now!

kidsonearth.life   kidsonearth.world

Click Below for Another Book In Each Series

senseipublishing.com/KoE_SERIES senseipublishing.com/KoE_Wildlife_SERIES

KoE EnEspañol

senseipublishing.com/KoE_SERIES_SPANISH

www.senseipublishing.com

Join Our Publishing Journey!

If you would like to receive FUTURE FREE BOOKS and get to know us better, please click www.senseipublishing.com and join our newsletter by entering your email address in the pop-up box.

Follow Our Blog: senseipauldavid.ca

Follow/Like/Subscribe: Facebook, Instagram, YouTube: @senseipublishing

Scan the QR Code with your phone or tablet to follow us on social media:

Like / Subscribe / Follow

Introduction

Welcome to the amazing world of the Atlantic spotted dolphin! This exciting book will take you on a journey to learn all about these incredible creatures. From their unique markings to the way they hunt for their food, you will learn 30 facts about the Atlantic spotted dolphins of Portugal. So, strap in and get ready to explore the wonderful world of these amazing mammals

This species is one of the most common dolphins seen in the area.

Atlantic spotted dolphins have a unique spotted pattern on their bodies, which helps them stand out in the water.

These dolphins typically travel in small pods of up to 20 individuals.

Atlantic spotted dolphins are carnivorous and feed on a variety of fish and squid.

These dolphins can dive up to 200 meters in search of food.

Atlantic spotted dolphins are highly intelligent and can use tools to help them hunt for food.

Atlantic spotted dolphins are social animals and often travel in large groups.

These dolphins are capable of using echolocation to detect food, prey, and obstacles in the water.

These dolphins often use play and socialization to strengthen bonds between individuals.

.

This species can reach speeds of up to 30 kilometers per hour.

The female Atlantic spotted dolphin gives birth to one calf every two to three years.

The Pygmy Slow Loris has a long-life span, with some individuals living up to 12 years in the wild.

The calves remain with their mothers for up to four years.

Atlantic spotted dolphins are curious and often approach boats and people in the water.

The Atlantic spotted dolphin is one of the few dolphin species that can jump out of the water.

The Atlantic spotted dolphin is a vulnerable species and is threatened by fishing and habitat destruction.

The Atlantic spotted dolphin is well adapted to living in the waters off of Portugal and the Azores.

35

These dolphins are active hunters and will often work Together to catch their prey.

The Atlantic spotted dolphin is an intelligent species and can learn from experience.

These dolphins are very social and will often stay together for life.

The Atlantic spotted dolphin is a highly vocal species and can make a variety of sounds.

These dolphins have a complex social structure and will often recognize individual members of their species.

Atlantic spotted dolphins have a wide range of diets and will often eat whatever is available in the area.

The Pygmy Slow Loris has a unique way of defending itself - it produces a special toxin from glands in its elbows that can be used to ward off predators.

This species is very active and can swim up to 40 kilometers in a single day.

Atlantic spotted dolphins are very social and often will form pods with other species of dolphins.

.

These dolphins use a variety of sounds to communicate with one another.

55

Atlantic spotted dolphins are very acrobatic and can often be seen doing flips and other tricks in the water.

Atlantic spotted dolphins often use vocalizations to coordinate their hunting activities.

These dolphins can live up to 40 years in the wild to living in the waters off of Portugal.

Conclusion

The Atlantic spotted dolphin is an amazing creature that inhabits the waters of Portugal and the Azores. This book has taught you 30 facts about these incredible animals. From their unique markings to the way they hunt, you now know more about the Atlantic spotted dolphin of Portugal. So the next time you're out on the water, keep an eye out for these amazing dolphins!

Thank you for reading this book!

If you found this book helpful, I would be grateful if you would **post an honest review on Amazon** so this book can reach other supportive readers like you!

All you need to do is digitally flip to the back and leave your review. Or visit amazon.com/author/senseipauldavid click the correct book cover and click on the blue link next to the yellow stars that say, "Customer reviews."

As always…

It's a great day to be alive!

Get/Share Our FREE eBooks Now!

kidsonearth.life

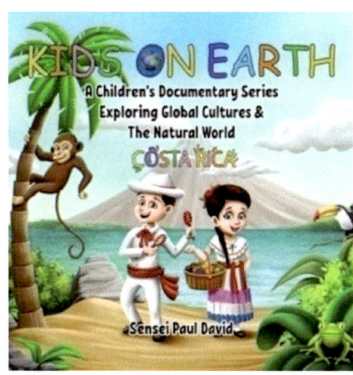

kidsonearth.world

Click Below for Another Book In Each Series

senseipublishing.com/KoE_SERIES senseipublishing.com/KoE_Wildlife_SERIES

KoE EnEspañol

senseipublishing.com/KoE_SERIES_SPANISH

www.senseipublishing.com

www.senseipublishing.com

@senseipublishing
#senseipublishing

\Check out our **recommendations** for other books for adults & kids plus other great resources by visiting
www.senseipublishing.com/resources/

Join Our Publishing Journey!

If you would like to receive FREE BOOKS and special offers, please visit www.senseipublishing.com and join our newsletter by entering your email address in the pop-up box

Follow Our Engaging Blog NOW!

senseipauldavid.ca

Get Our FREE Books Today!

Click & Share the Links Below

FREE Kids Books
lifeofbailey.senseipublishing.com
kidsonearth.senseipublishing.com
FREE Self-Development Book

senseiselfdevelopment.senseipublishing.com

FREE BONUS!!!
Experience Over 25 FREE Engaging Guided Meditations!

Prized Skills & Practices for Adults & Kids. Help Restore Deep Sleep, Lower Stress, Improve Posture, Navigate Uncertainty & More.

Download the Free Insight Timer App and click the link below:
http://insig.ht/sensei_paul

About Sensei Publishing

Sensei Publishing commits itself to help people of all ages transform into better versions of themselves by providing high-quality and research-based self-development books with an emphasis on mental health and guided meditations. Sensei Publishing offers well-written e-books, audiobooks, paperbacks, and online courses that simplify complicated but practical topics in line with its mission to inspire people toward positive transformation.

It's a great day to be alive!

About the Author

I create simple & transformative eBooks & Guided Meditations for Adults & Children proven to help navigate uncertainty, solve niche problems & bring families closer together.

I'm a former finance project manager, private pilot, jiu-jitsu instructor, musician & former University of Toronto Fitness Trainer. I prefer a science-based approach to focus on these & other areas in my life to stay humble & hungry to evolve. I hope you enjoy my work and I'd love to hear your feedback.
- It's a great day to be alive!
Sensei Paul David

Scan & Follow/Like/Subscribe: Facebook, Instagram, YouTube: @senseipublishing

Scan using your phone/iPad camera for social media
Visit us at www.senseipublishing.com and sign up for our newsletter to learn more about our exciting books and to experience our FREE Guided Meditations for Kids & Adults.

www.ingramcontent.com/pod-product-compliance
Lightning Source LLC
Chambersburg PA
CBRC090901080526
44587CB00008B/164